POGO

by

Walt Kelly

FANTAGRAPHICS BOOKS

7563 Lake City Way NE
Seattle WA 98115

Edited by Tom Spurgeon
Design and Production by David Lasky
Thanks to Steve Thompson, Bill Blackbeard, and Rick Norwood
for historical and archival assistance
Published by Gary Groth and Kim Thompson

First Fantagraphics Books edition: June, 1998
10 9 8 7 6 5 4 3 2 1

ISBN: 1-56097-342-0

Printed in the U.S.A.

Checkers and Other Kinds of Bull, in Assorted Shades of White, Blue, and (Heaven Forfend) Red

By R.C. Harvey

As we flock trippingly to the end of the century, we occasionally glance back over our shoulders, as is our wont, to the beginning of this madcap millennium, looking wistfully for some clue as to where we might first have started to stray from the high road of exalted purpose to the primrose path of hanky-panky in high places that so distinguishes the politics of the *fin de siècle*. What was the "first cause," the initiating stub against which we tested a toe and from which we never quite recovered, descending, instead, further and further into the maelstrom of sensationalism and titillation that, by now, the journalistic media mistake for public affairs reporting? Wont not, I trow, it turns out we have a lot for which to blame Teddy Roosevelt.

Stuffed animals, for instance. "From Teddy Bears to Beanie Babies" might well be the slogan for the century — from trivia to trivia in popular culture. But behind the elevation of the common man (and woman) to eminence in our culture is, surely, the expansion of the primary election.

The Presidential primary is now a media institution that goes on without let or cease in relentless disregard for the calendar by which Presidents are supposed to be elected only once every four years. Until Theodore Roosevelt made the "preferential primary," or "direct primary," an issue in his 1912 bid for the nomination of the Republican Party, most delegates to the quadrennial gatherings of the political parties were selected through state conventions of political parties or confabulations of the backroom power brokers. But Roosevelt needed to change that because it was clear that the backroom boys were bent on nominating the incumbent, William Howard Taft. Taft had been Roosevelt's own

choice as successor when he had declined to run again for the Presidency in 1908 (having served almost two full terms), and the two had been the best of friends; but Taft had fallen so short of TR's hopes for him as to become a virtual enemy of the old Rough Rider, which, to Roosevelt, was the same as being an enemy of the country. Aflame with patriotic fervor (not to mention seething with disappointment at Taft's failures), Roosevelt announced that he would make a run for the Republican nomination. "My hat is in the ring," he proclaimed, giving American political life an enduring phrase, the first of the two he bequeathed to his countrymen in the 1912 battle.

To unseat the Taft juggernaut, Roosevelt went straight to the people. His clarion appeal urged voters to demand that their states install "direct" primary elections as the best way of giving people a voice in government. His popularity was such that six states inaugurated primaries that spring, bringing to a total of thirteen the states with direct primaries that enabled the party faithful to circumvent the dictates of the backroom bosses. TR got most of the convention delegates in those thirteen states: 388 delegates were at stake, and he collected 281 of them, soundly defeating Taft. But that scarcely decided the issue: the convention would have 1,078 delegates, most of them chosen by the old method — most of them pledged to Taft. Still, Roosevelt arrived at the convention in Chicago prepared to contest several state delegations, and if he had won the day, he could have secured the nomination. Alas, the convention machinery was in the hands of the Taft forces, and TR lost his bid. His popularity among large numbers of delegates, however, was so great that they all met again two months later, formed the Progressive Party, and nominated Roosevelt. In the ensuing three-way race for the White House, Roosevelt's candidacy divided the Republican vote, and the Democrat candidate, Woodrow Wilson, emerged victorious.

But the direct primary as a means of selecting delegates to political conventions had edged into the nation's political life. And it would eventually — by the time we reached the other end of the century — prevail nearly everywhere and would consume the attention and energy of every Presidential aspirant for years before Election Year.

Now, that other phrase. When Roosevelt arrived in Chicago in June 1912 for the Republican convention, he was, as is usual with political figures, stalked wherever he went by a phalanx of reporters. One of them asked him how he was feeling, a sort of general welfare question. And TR responded, smiling in remembrance of his hunting experiences: "I'm feeling," he said, "like a bull moose." The next morning, "Bull Moose" appeared in huge letters in newspaper headlines. The image captured the popular fancy (irrespective of the probable fact that few of the reading public had ever even seen a bull moose or could image how one might feel under any given set of circumstances). Campaign buttons were quickly manufactured sporting the antlered figure. The idea, the spirit, of this woodland giant seemed to embody a kind of defiant robustness, exactly what Roosevelt represented. The Progressive Party was quickly dubbed "the Bull Moose Party," and supporters of TR were "Bull-moosers." And that brings us to *Pogo* in the fall of 1952, into which Walt Kelly introduces a bull moose on October 6 (10/6) in the midst of the Eisenhower-Stevenson election campaign for the Presidency.

Although renowned in later years for the political satire of his strip, Kelly had only begun exploring this dimension of possibilities in 1952. He would plumb it to the fullest by the summer of 1953, but it's entirely possible that Kelly's bull moose is foraging through the month of October without any satirical purpose whatsoever. Kelly could do that — abandon satire in favor of plotless meanderings and comedic whimsies created solely for the sake of simple, unadorned hilarity. That was his wont, after all. And it was a wont that produced some of the strip's most satisfying moments, too. There had been enough of those moments to persuade the inky-fingered fraternity at the National Cartoonists Society to bestow upon Kelly its highest accolade: he'd been named Outstanding Cartoonist of the Year for 1951, and that was before he'd betrayed any pronounced satirical tendencies in the political vein.

THE DISHON. TOM MALONE

ARF

Still, having embraced the 1952 Presidential election by getting Pogo drafted as a candidate that summer, Kelly might be expected to take up political satire with a vengeance in the fall once the campaign heated up. We are therefore tempted to look for deeper meanings in the sudden appearance of a bull moose, unemployed since "19-ought-12."

The parallels between the campaigns of 1912 and 1952 are numerous enough to offer several possibilities. Republican candidate Dwight Eisenhower, five-star general and architect of World War II's victory over Hitler in Europe, had been opposed for the nomination by Robert A. Taft, grandson of the Taft who Roosevelt sought to dethrone. In short, by a miraculously poetic turn of events, Robert Taft occupied a position in the 1952 Republican convention roughly similar to that held by TR in 1912. But Robert Taft had announced his post-convention support for Ike, so Kelly's bull moose was probably not intended to evoke him. At the summer's convention of Democrats, Estes Kefauver had been unhorsed in his race for the nomination in almost exactly the way Roosevelt had been dispensed with in 1912. But he had slipped from public view by the time the campaign heated up in the fall. Then there's Harry Truman.

Truman's Presidential career is an exact parallel of Roosevelt's: both were Vice Presidents when a President died, and, after serving most of that four-year term, both ran for and were elected to the Presidency in their own right. Both served nearly two full terms; both could, however, run for a "third" term because neither had been elected to the office twice. Both, initially, declined to run for another four-year term. TR reconsidered after he'd been out of office for a term (from 1908 until 1912); Truman never had such second thoughts. But he was an active campaigner in the cause of his party's candidate, Adlai Stevenson. Stevenson, erstwhile governor of Illinois, was Truman's hand-picked heir in the Democrat Party. Truman was to

Stevenson precisely what Roosevelt had been to Taft in the 1908 election. Given Kelly's support of Truman in the 1948 election, we might suppose that the cartoonist's introduction of a bull moose into Pogo's election commentary was a veiled nudge to Truman to throw himself into the fray for a "third" term just as TR had done. Maybe. But that's quite a stretch in search of satirical import.

Truman's engagement on Stevenson's behalf churned up the muck on the campaign trail. Having won the White House in 1948 by giving the Republicans "hell," Truman tried the same whistle-stop, tub-thumping techniques again. Ike, Truman said, has "endorsed a reign of terror by slander — the indiscriminate slaughter of the good name of one's opponents" (a reference to Eisenhower's countenancing of Senator Joseph McCarthy's scurrilous commie-hunting campaign). Ike, Truman went on, has "uttered crass equivocations designed to win the votes — and the contributions — of the [Southern] millionaires" and "is spreading false and slanderous charges that the Democrat Party is soft on communism — a fantastic smear technique." And, he said, "the Republican Party and the Republican candidate have waged one of the lowest street-gutter campaigns that I have ever seen." Truman also managed to accuse Eisenhower of anti-Semitism. Truman was hardly a voice of quiet reason that season, and the overall tenor of the campaign was consequently strident and bitter.

When Kelly invoked memories of the Bull Moose that TR had been, he was more than likely simply washing his hands of the whole mess in disgust, his liberal sensibilities thoroughly offended. The antlered allusion, in other words, was to a long-lost dream — a wish, even, for some way to escape the nastiness of the 1952 campaign. It wasn't exactly TR that was being invoked. Or Taft or Truman or any other specific personage. It was, rather, the example TR set of showing a way to evade politics as usual. As the moose himself says, he has been unemployed since 1912; the ideal, perforce, has not been much adhered to. But, says the moose (10/10), "this presidential race between two major candidates is the opportunity of the *masses* … to sneak into the White House an' hold it against *all com-*

ers." In unfurling the image of the Bull Moose, Kelly was crying out for the Presidency to be somehow taken away from politicians with all their electioneering mendacity and mud-throwing. Still, while seeming to call for a plague on both the political houses, Kelly was both realist and liberal: the White House, he has Pogo remind us, is occupied by someone who might be "breakin' it in for a friend."

In a way, Kelly turned his back on the political issues of the day that were being chewed over so savagely in the campaign: rather than participate in the process, Pogo decamps, disguised as "a runaway gal orphan" accompanied by his faithful canine companion, Beauregard Bugleboy the Bloodhound. Conservative Harold Gray's Little Orphan Annie and her dog Sandy were not at all reticent in the arena of political comment, so there's some irony in Kelly's choice of parody vehicle, but the "runaway" metaphor certainly reflects a certain rueful lack of interest in the ongoing political scrap.

But Kelly's choice here was a matter of some practicality, too. In part, his decision was doubtless dictated by the uncertainties of any political campaign, the volatility of the issues and their transitory nature: the issues lofted on one day are often out of sight on the next. Drawing his strip four-six weeks ahead of publication dates, Kelly could scarcely know which issues to pick for satiric exploitation. With bad luck, whatever he picked might be off the political map by the time the strips commenting on it were published.

The biggest scandal of the campaign, for example, surfaced and was blown out of the water all in a fortnight. Richard Nixon, Eisenhower's running mate, was accused in late September of supplementing his income with a slush fund supplied to him by Southern California millionaires. Nixon lost no time in securing television broadcast time to explain the fund. Many politicians had similar funding arrangements — even Adlai Stevenson; so the issue was created solely by Nixon's zealous Democrat opponents who inflated it to scandalous proportions. Nixon made a persuasive case for himself a week after the story broke: this was the fabled "Checkers speech," one of the most extraordinary political performances in American politics.

For thirty minutes on nationwide television, Nixon proclaimed his innocence. (Checkers, for those not paying attention, was the name Nixon's daughter Tricia had given to a cocker spaniel pup that an enthusiastic supporter had shipped to the family — *gratis*, an out and out gift. Or, it was strenuously implied, a bribe of some sort. In revealing this act of political bribery, Nixon said, "You know kids: they love the dog, and, regardless of what they say about it, we're going to keep it." Such innocence in those dear dead days of yore.) So convincing was Nixon that Ike promptly embraced him, reinstating him as his choice for Vice President, and the body politic presumably forgot all about it in a few days. If Kelly had chosen to comment on the incident, by the time his comment appeared, it would seem irrelevant.

The other big issues of the day were the Korean War and the alleged communist infiltration of government. People wanted the Korean conflict to cease; and they wanted someone to clean communists out of all areas of American life. Simple as that.

Eisenhower, perceived not only as a wartime hero but as a military genius, capitalized on his stature and announced that, if elected, he would "go to Korea" in person. In making this startling statement, Ike strenuously implied not only that he had the expertise to end the War single-handedly but that somehow Truman, who had been a politician longer than he'd been a soldier, had bungled the whole business by failing to understand the military aspects of the situation.

Truman, naturally, boiled over: "If he knows how to cure the situation in Korea," he fumed, "it's his duty to come and tell me how to do it and save lives right now." Good point.

When Eisenhower won the election (it was a landslide: he had 53% of a record voter turnout, capturing 442 of the 531 electoral votes; Stevenson even lost in his home state), Truman's telegrammed congratulations concluded with a sly reference to Ike's campaign pledge: "The Independence [the Presidential aircraft] will be at your disposal if you still desire to go to Korea." Ike, steaming in turn that Truman would think his promise was merely a campaign stunt, wired back: "Any suitable transport plane that one of the services could make available will be satisfactory for my planned trip to Korea."

Ike went to Korea in December. And the following summer, a cease fire prevailed in Korea while all parties began sitting at a conference table (where they remained for decades in the longest unresolved peace negotiation in history).

Kelly made no references to the Korean War. Again, his reticence is understandable: wars are not good subjects for satire while they are in progress. During October, another 1,278 American soldiers died in a single week's action. The U.S. death toll reached 21,471 that month, with 89,263 wounded, 10,793 missing, and 1,868 in prisoner of war camps. Nothing funny about that.

Wisconsin's Senator Joe McCarthy, the self-appointed crusader against communists in government, master of the smear and character assassin extraordinary, had secured for himself an appointment that made him the national watchdog in perpetuity: he was now chairman of the Senate Permanent Investigating Committee. A "permanent" committee. So dire was the communist threat that the Senate deemed it necessary to install one of its own at the head of a permanent investigatory body, dedicated to ferreting out communists wherever they might secret themselves. Forever. For publicity hound McCarthy, it was a dream come true.

Not everything was going McCarthy's way, though. Various members of the Senate had voiced doubts about his fitness to serve, and he himself was under investigation by that body's Privileges and Elections Subcommittee. Among the suspicious aspects of the old buccaneer's career was his bank account, which seemed to have swollen since he began his fight against communism.

Although the scowling Senator was able to keep the issue of communists in the public eye, Kelly almost ignored it during the campaign months. His only reference to communists took the form of a couple of encore appearances by the cowbird comrades on 10/27 and 11/1. But a few months later the witch-hunters of McCarthy's stripe would be featured players in the strip.

Kelly never set out to record reactions to every

aspect of American life. But if he passed over current events in popular culture, he did not neglect the art of his medium. He continued to exhibit a dazzling mastery of the form, blending word and picture to achieve a meaning neither embodies alone without the other. On 10/11, for instance, we have an antique chestnut of a joke but a vivid demonstration of the way pictures add meaning to words and vice versa in the best examples of the form.

The same strip displays in miniature Kelly's penchant for a kind of loopy, leap-frogging plot development. The conversation leaps from one misapprehended meaning to another, moving the "story" closer and closer to a punchline with every leap: Houn'dog's opening remark reminds us of the moose's prolixity, and his anecdote about getting his horns stuck in a taxi doorway leads to Pogo's observation about an orchestra, then Houn'dog's remark about a traveling band, ending with the visual pun about the broadening effects of travel.

Kelly managed whole storylines with the same blithe disregard for the purely sequential logic that guides most narratives. The so-called "story" that begins 1/16, for example, lurches forward, day by day, with a lyric illogic all its own, creating eddies of comedy at every turn. Seminole Sam, the swamp's resident con-man, initiates the sequence by proposing that he and his colleagues corner the market on water — without which, he points out, soap manufacturers would go broke. Howland Owl then goes Sam one better, opting for "dry water," but Porkypine's Uncle Baldwin puts his finger on the absolutely indispensable element in the whole enterprise of housewifery — dirt — an ingredient he and Churchy La Femme try to keep secret while they also try to sell it by the box. Once Owl discovers the secret, he conjures up an advertising empire with himself at the head, a notion that quickly leads to a spoof of television programming as well as marketing when Owl equates his product, dirt, with television's most visible product, gossip. And this sets the stage for the arrival of Mole MacCarony with his passion for cleanliness. It would be impossible to say, however, that Kelly himself envisioned this tidy outcome when he first brought Seminole Sam back on stage to try to sell water.

Along the way, Kelly gets in a few jabs at political matters. On 1/21, the day after Eisenhower's inauguration, he slights the incoming administration when Uncle Baldwin reminds his co-conspirators in the water deal that the Republicans' traditional high tariff policies would prevent importing the Canadian half of Niagara Falls at anything like a reasonable rate. And when Owl and Sam break up their partnership, the ensuing verbal exchange goes from million through billion and trillion, arriving eventually at vermillion, which permits Kelly an allusion to the communist issue (2/18). Finally, on 2/23, Baldwin's free demonstration gives the witch-hunting, dirt-digging Deacon Mushrat a dose of his own medicine (foreshadowing the outcome to Kelly's attack on Joe McCarthy later in the year).

Throughout the months that begin unrolling a few pages to the right, Kelly veers off into vaudevillian slapstick at the slightest provocation. The water-dirt-gossip sequence we just reviewed bubbles over with this tendency. But the most satisfyingly sustained sample of it takes place the first week in January (1/5-10), when Owl and Churchy think they've pulled Uncle Baldwin's head off. (And the wordplay with "inscrutable" and "unscrewed" is delicious.) Nearly every day, Kelly does a complete reverse, beginning with one set of assumptions and then neatly upsetting them by the last panel. The concluding strip (1/10) is simply a perfect conclusion to the sequence. Owl's expressions in this series are priceless — in the last panels of 1/10 and 1/7 and in the first panel of 1/9, particularly.

In this sequence — as in many others — Kelly deftly exploits the verbal-visual character of the medium. The pictures are virtually meaningless without the accompanying words. And vice versa. But Kelly is also marvelously adroit in simply manipulating language for comic effect. Again in a vaudevillian mode, on 1/16, Churchy's "Where?" is a quip for which Sam's opening statement is a classic setup. But the exchange between Baldwin and Churchy in the last panel of 1/22 is a comic notch above slapstick, fraught with nonsense that might be significant. And on 2/11, we find both classic vaudeville and veiled significance in Sam's third panel question: he's just labeled himself a fool.

Another kind of verbal manipulation occurs on the day after the Election. Since syndicated comic strips are produced several weeks before they appear in print, Kelly could scarcely know who would win. But he manages to convey the impression that he does by having Churchy pick out the letters in the winner's name — letters both Stevenson and *Eisenhower* have in common. (This is mostly an in-group joke with his cartooning brethren. Kelly could have manufactured two strips for issuing on this date, one announcing Stevenson the winner; the other, Eisenhower. But he chose to deal with the question in a way that demonstrated his own cleverness at surmounting the difficulty.)

Hilarious as all this verbal hijinks is, it's Kelly's blending of the verbal and the visual that reveals his consummate command of the medium. Vital as the verbiage is to the broad comedy of such vaude-

villian turns as the week of January 5th, the humor of that sequence could not exist in purely verbal terms: the pictures did not simply add to the humor, they completed it.

But Kelly could yoke pictures to words for other effects, too. Sometimes the visual element carries the biggest load: when Porky departs the strip on 11/26, even the white space of the speech balloon (and that solitary falling leaf, clinging to its edge) is enlisted to evoke an empty feeling of sadness, a visual cue that completes the mood suggested by the sagging shouldered postures of the other characters in the panel.

Porky's predicament initiates one of the most unusual sequences in *Pogo*. For the next week, it rains in the swamp. A continuous torrent of rain. And rain, as Will Eisner demonstrated repeatedly in the long run of *The Spirit*, conveys a pervasive sense of gloom and sadness. And then Kelly gets Pogo and Albert lost, too, which adds hopelessness to the mix of atmospherics (the last panel in 12/2 particularly). This is prelude to the Christmas season and one of the most affecting of Kelly's celebrations of the occasion in the strip.

A classic bit of vaudevillian humor chases the clouds away on 12/9: "You is found!" yells Willow McWisper as he "finds" the lost duo. With McWisper to guide them through the gloom, Pogo and Albert set off to find Porky. Meanwhile, back home, Churchy readies the troops for the ritual recital of "Deck the Halls with Boston Charlie." Kelly alternates between rehearsal scenes and the lost-and-found expedition, keeping both the celebratory season and the dire situation before us. And then on Christmas Eve, in one of Kelly's triumphs of visual-verbal blending in the service of story — in fact, here, the blend may be the story — the lost trio returns, guided by the glow of a firefly in the night, just in time to share in the "anyule" greeting. Three folks guided by a light in the sky at Christmas — a familiar image? And so the lost are found. Has a biblical ring to it, eh? Seldom did Kelly blend word and picture for poetry as resonant with allusive meaning as this.

But the day after Christmas, Kelly reminds us

with a tirade from Deacon Mushrat that life beyond the holiday is not so merry.

In real life, too, the Yuletide news that year was not all sugar plums cavorting in kiddies' craniums. In the holiday outing of the television program *This Is Show Business*, one of the hosts, playwright George S. Kaufman, rattled network executives by rousing the ire of some of the audience. In his familiar curmudgeonly manner, Kaufman said, "Let's make this one program on which nobody sings *Silent Night.*" Most of the program's viewers accepted this observation in the spirit in which it was offered — as a protest against the overuse of Christmas carols for commercial purposes. But the CBS switchboard lit up like a Christmas tree with a fringe element protest against Kaufman's "irreligious remark." Panicky, CBS fired Kaufman and began searching desperately for a replacement. To their credit, newsman John Daly, and comedians Garry Moore and Fred Allen declined. (Allen, with his usual acerbic wit: "This thing is ridiculous. There are only two good wits on television, Groucho Marx and George S. Kaufman. With Kaufman gone, TV is half-witted.") Steve Allen took the job, but it lasted only a few weeks. Once the panic of the moment dissipated, CBS thought better of its hasty action and reinstated Kaufman.

Still, the incident reveals much about the atmosphere of the country at the time. Not so different from the way it is now, a cynic might say. But in those days, the air was infected with Red Scare vapors, too. The fear had some basis in reality, after all. When the Soviet Union acquired the secret of the atomic bomb, many Americans were terrified of the possible consequences. And when it was discovered that there was a ring of spies passing atomic secrets to the Russians — and that one spy, Alger Hiss, was actually a highly placed government official — the basis was established for the Age of Suspicion. Communists must be lurking everywhere in government, a paranoid notion that McCarthy would make a career of fanning into a conflagration of self-promotion. In January 1953, Julius and Ethel Rosenberg, the couple at the center of the spy ring, were scheduled to die in the electric chair at Sing

Sing prison, proclaiming their innocence to the end. In various corners of the country, sympathetic souls marched in protest, and the execution was postponed again and again until summer.

With the elections over, the news engines of the nation turned once more to the sensations to be found in the search for communists in places of influence in American life. Investigatory bodies pried into everything. Scores of "disloyal" Americans, it was discovered, had infiltrated the official staff of the United Nations. Even more startling, most of these had come directly from government service in Washington. Among the results of the hearings conducted by the House Un-American Activities Committee was the publication in California of a self-proclaimed anti-Red magazine called *Alert*. Listing the names of 522 Hollywood film industry figures that had been culled from HUAAC's records, this document was the West Coast blacklist companion to New York's *Counterattack*. Congress was investigating schools and colleges, too, fingering this teacher and that as a "communist sympathizer." And McCarthy turned his attention to the State Department's Voice of America operation. Conducting his hearings on television, the chivvying chairman of the Senate Investigation Committee clearly enjoyed being in the spotlight as he needled and wheedled the witnesses, often brow-beating them into frustrated silence. Seminole Sam's behavior in *Pogo* on 2/12 would look familiar to anyone who had tuned in to the McCarthy hearings.

Significant numbers of government employees whom McCarthy had pursued so avidly for the past two years would turn out, in the long run, to be innocent of all subversive connection save a long-expired youthful interest in socialism or communism during the destitute 1930s. But by the time their guiltlessness was established, their careers and reputations had been ruined. Kelly, acutely conscious of the evil being wrought in these machinations, returned to the subject in March 1953.

Months before, he had introduced the Boy Bird Watchers in the strip as the allegorical equivalent of the witch-hunting investigatory groups that devoted endless hours to turning over moss-encrusted rocks looking for un-American slugs and other underground agents. He established the hapless bat brothers as permanent members of the club and put the censorious Deacon Mushrat at the head of the bumbling band. This disreputable bunch appeared most recently in the strip during September, when the cowbirds joined their ranks. Kelly brings

back them back in this volume's reprints on 1/15. Just a single, one-panel appearance in the middle of a month devoted otherwise to matters having little to do with bird watching. The Deacon's furtive crouch shrouds this cameo appearance with sinister import despite the vaudevillian chatter of the bats at his back. It is an unforgettably ominous moment in the strip, an artful prelude to future events that Kelly was clearly already mulling over.

When the Deacon returns on Monday 3/2, Kelly has prepared the stage for the arrival of Mole MacCarony. Howland Owl has established his television program on "Dirt." Kelly intends us to perceive "dirt," partly, as "gossip" — innuendo and rumor — the sort of pseudo-information McCarthy was so adept at dealing in. (Note how adroitly the word-playing Kelly turns "columnist" into "calumnist," one who, we assume, traffics in "calumny" — i.e., false statement; 2/25 and 3/7.) That Kelly sees television as a culpable partner in McCarthyism seems clear; and television is Mole's first platform on his way to

power. But his brief debut on Owl's program (3/6) is but an incident in his career.

Mole comes to the swamp to help with the spring bird watching (communist hunting). And in portraying Mole as fanatic about sanitary conditions, Kelly perfectly captures the righteous fervor of the witch-hunters. "Bacteria from all over infect the pure air of our land," Mole cries (3/9). But Mole's ability to discover impurities is seriously in doubt: the Deacon says he has "a keen eye," but Kelly shows him bumping blindly into a tree in the very next panel (3/4). Kelly is pulling no punches: he makes sure we understand that "bird watching" is being conducted by people who aren't very perceptive.

Perfect though Mole seems as a satirical vehicle for Kelly's attack on the Red Hunt, the character is too much a buffoon to stand in for the gimlet-eyed Senator from Wisconsin, who Kelly sees as a frighteningly diabolic figure in American life. He can manipulate Mole for laughs, thereby ridiculing the witch-hunters; but he needs something much more grimly threatening, too. And in the next volume of this series, we'll see how he meets the challenge with the masterpiece of his career as a satirist and cartoonist.

Later in the run of *Pogo*, Kelly attracted considerable notice among the more fervent of his fans for the names he scrawled on the sides of the flat-bottomed boats his characters poled around in. Initially, the boats bore the names of cities — "City of Nashville"; and that provoked no curiosity. But when people's names showed up, some of Kelly's most dedicated readers might be expected to want to know who these folks are.

Steve Thompson, editor and publisher of *The Fort Mudge Most*, the official magazine of the Pogo Fan Club, shared his speculation on the matter with me. (A six-issue subscription is $25; Spring Hollow Books, 6908 Wentworth Avenue South, Richfield, MN 55423.) Some considerable evidence suggests, Thompson opines, that names on the boat were promotional stunts. Not at first, mayhap, but eventually. Syndicate salesmen urged Kelly to put on the boat the names of newspaper executives at newspapers they were going to call on, hoping the official would be flattered into buying the strip; or, with Kelly's connivance, the salesmen were empowered to promise an editor that his name would go on the boat as soon as his paper bought the strip.

Probably a wholly accurate speculation. Some of those named were Kelly drinking companions, but many were newspaper folks — professional associates perhaps, client newspaper executives probably. But who, specifically, were they? Much as I'd like to solve these modest mysteries in these introductory notes, I'm afraid I can't. Not with every name anyhow. I don't know them all. Moreover, eventually, there will be too many of them: identifying them all would consume pages and convert these prefaces into full-scale encyclopedias. In 1952-53, however, not every boat is emblazoned with a name. The practice had not yet become a compulsion with Kelly. So by way of an exemplary exposition, let me tackle just one of the names.

"The Hon. Walter Lister" showed up on a boat about a year ago (January 9, 1952). Lister was managing editor of the *Philadelphia Bulletin*, and he and Kelly may have enjoyed a convivial professional association — or maybe he had just bought *Pogo* for the *Bulletin*. A few years later, however, Kelly might not have honored Lister with this kind of genial publicity. In 1955 in the March issue of *The Bulletin of the American Society of Newspaper Editors*, Lister wrote an article in which he said that "comics, once regarded as a specific for all circulation ills, are now the sick chicks of the newspaper business." He went on to cite a survey in one city that showed readership of the funnies had fallen off by fifteen percent. Television was the reason, Lister continued: it had lured readers away from the back pages of newspapers where the comics usually ran. Then he quoted from two more readership surveys, both conducted in small towns in Alabama — one town that didn't, yet, have television; one that did. In the former, comics were read by 68 percent of the paper's readers; in the latter, by only 31 percent. Lister's notions received wider currency when *Time* magazine reported his findings. The potential damage to newspaper comics was enormous: Lister had undermined the very *raison d'etre* for comics. News-

papers published comics in order to attract readers. And if comics weren't being read any more, they could be discarded. The entire cartooning profession was threatened.

Within a week or so of the publication of Lister's article, the Newspaper Comics Council was able to refute his contentions. The surveys he cited were flawed, for one thing; and other surveys, casting nets over much wider audiences, showed that readership of the comics had fallen only about five percent as television had come on the scene — a decline paralleled almost exactly by a fall-off in readership in all departments of the newspaper. Moreover, comics readership was still higher than the readership of any other department by 15-20%. The episode faded quickly, but it's doubtful that Kelly would have put Lister's name on a boat afterwards.

And, speaking of names, who, you might ask, is Kathryn B., the person with the Hallowe'en birthday to whom a drifting bug refers on 12/8? Kelly had a daughter named Kathryn Barbara; she died while still an infant. I haven't been able to find out when, exactly; but given the poignant reference on 12/8, I suspect that she was born in the fall of 1952 and died within a few weeks. *Uncle Pogo's So-So Stories*, not a reprint volume but a book of original material, was published early in 1953, and it is dedicated to the mother of Kathryn Barbara with a poem. That poem appears first in the strip, recited by Porky on 3/13 and again the next day.

Another mystery in the strips herein is provoked by Churchy's frequently voiced desire to journey to "the Bermoothes" to watch "the onions and the eels." Dunno what all that means. Could be, though, it has reference to Stevenson, who went to Barbados to recover from the campaign. And there's an old story about Stevenson that I like. Reportedly, he once remarked (after an election campaign I believe) that what he wanted to do most was to sit under the shade of a tree, drinking lemonade and watching the people dance. Onions and eels? Maybe not.

Elsewhere in the pages to the right, you will find Uncle Baldwin attired in a funny hat and a full-length coat, probably of the trench species. Despite

the fact that he is naked underneath the coat (having lost his quills), don't make too much of this: the flasher craze didn't come along for another decade or two. And — tempting though it may be to claim that Baldwin's attentions to Miz Mam'selle Hepzibah invoke Bill Clinton's conduct with lady acquaintances, that is scarcely the case. Kelly was clever but not prescient. Still, it's nice to see that women of Hepzibah's generation knew how to deal with mashers (1/28).

But maybe we shouldn't take such things all that seriously. As Porky said about life itself, "It ain't nohow permanent."

The Cast

In our continuing effort to learn just how many characters Kelly employed in the swamp, here are listed, in the order of appearance, those who made their first appearance in this volume (bringing the cast total to 127):

Bull Moose (not, apparently, Uncle Antler, since he's never named)
Baldwin (Porky's uncle)
Lump Lou the Fat Frog
Willow McWisper
Miz Angleworm
Mole MacCarony
Mrockthorton

As a footnote, I must report that alert reader David C. Kopaska-Merkel wrote to tell me that the third bat's name is not "Bilmildered" but "Bemildred." Although the bat in question calls himself "Bewildered" on the first several times he introduces himself, he is later identified by another cast member (March 23, 1951) as "Bemildred." True, all too true.

OCTOBER 6, 1952

OCTOBER 7, 1952

OCTOBER 8, 1952

AS A *ORPHAN GAL*, YOU GOTTA USE A LOT OF *EX-PRESSIONS* LIKE: *JEEPING WHILKERS* AN' *WHEE JILLIKENS!*

ARF

THE DISHON. TOM MALONE

AN' *YOU*, AS A *DOG*, YOU GOTTA PRACTICE UP ON DEFENDIN' THE POOR LI'L ORPHAN... AT THE *DROP* OF A *STRANGE FOOT-FALL....*

JILKING WHEEZERS.'

BRISK UP! A-RISE! AND HOLLER IN A GREAT VOICE: *ARF! ARF!*

COPR. 1952 WALT KELLY

CATCH ON?

STICK AROUND! YOU DEFEND HER AT SEA. I'LL TAKE OVER ON LAND FROM NOW ON.

WHILLIKING JEEPERS, FELLERS.

OCTOBER 9, 1952

FRIENDS, I'M AN OLD *BULL MOOSER*... PLENTY OF EXPERIENCE IN THE CANDIDATURE LINE.... MUST OF RUN FOR *EVERYTHIN'* ONE TIME OR *A·NOTHER*.

COPR. 1952 WALT KELLY

RAN FOR THE BOSTON AN' MAINE *TRAIN* ONE TIME.... CAUGHT IT, TOO, AN' WOULD HAVE HAD IT STUFFED BUT THE LAW SAID IT WAS *UNDERSIZED* AN' I HAD TO THROW IT BACK.....*ALL* THE *WHOLE* WAY TO LYNN.

ANOTHER TIME I RAN FOR *DOG-CATCHER* ON THE LONG ISLAND TICKET.

WATCH YOUR LANGUAGE!

CALMLY! CALMLY! THE DOGCATCHER IS A LATE TRAIN CARRYIN' HOME LATE STRAYS AND WANDERIN' CELEBRANTS.

BESIDES *I* IS THE *DOG*... I SHOULD RESENT THINGS LIKE THAT AN' I *DON'T*.

AW, JEEPING WHILKERS FELLERS.

POGO

by Walt Kelly

OCTOBER 10, 1952

IT'S MY OPINION THAT THIS *PRESI-DENTIAL* RACE BETWEEN TWO MAJOR CANDIDATES IS THE **OPPORTUNITY** OF THE *MASSES.*

WOOP! WATCH IT! WHAT MASSES?

US MASSES OF **MOOSES.**

JEEPING WHILKERS, FELLERS.

ARF!

WHILE TWO **BIG BOYS** FIGHT EACH OTHER TO A **STAND-OFF,** US MASSES OF MOOSES CAN SNEAK INTO THE *WHITE HOUSE* AN' HOLD IT AGAINST **ALL COMERS!**

BUT A MAN IS ALREADY **IN** IT.

SKULLDUGGERY! WHAT'S *HE* DOIN' IN THERE?

EASY! EASY! HE MIGHT JUST BE BREAKIN' IT IN FOR A FRIEND.

OCTOBER 11, 1952

I'M WEARIN' THE ORPHAN'S WIG 'CAUSE *I'M* S'POSED TO TALK AN' *HE* USES UP ALL THE SPACE.

WENT TO THE **ELKS'** CONVENTION UP **NEW** YORK STATE WAY, BUT GOT STUCK IN A **TAXI** DOORWAY.

AN' THE CONVENTION WAS **OVER** AND I OWED **$4,319.50** ON THE CLOCK BY THE TIME THEY SPRUNG MY HORNS LOOSE.

YOU SURE DO HAVE HORNS ENOUGH TO START A SMALL ORCHESTRA.

YEH, YOU COULD FORM A GROUP OF **TRAVELIN'** MUSICIANS SINGLE HANDED.

WELL, THEY SAY TRAVEL *IS* BROADENING.

AN' *THAT* AIN'T EXACTLY WHAT *YOU* NEED.

OCTOBER 13, 1952

OCTOBER 14, 1952

4

OCTOBER 15, 1952

OCTOBER 16, 1952

OCTOBER 17, 1952

OCTOBER 18, 1952

OCTOBER 20, 1952

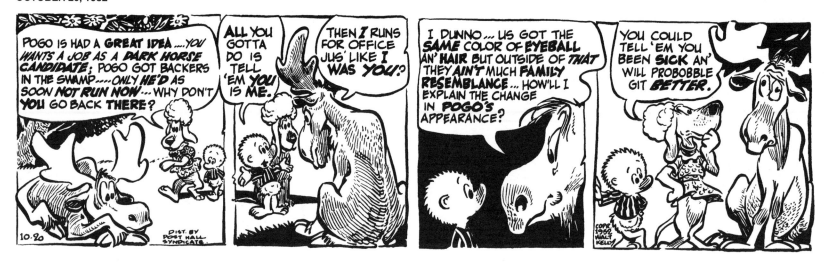

OCTOBER 21, 1952

OCTOBER 22, 1952

OCTOBER 23, 1952

8

OCTOBER 24, 1952

OCTOBER 25, 1952

OCTOBER 27, 1952

THE ONLY WAY TO VISIT MY **UNCLE BALDWIN** IS TO *DO* IT---- HE'S ALLUS COUNTIN' HIS **HAIR** AN' GITTIN' **BALDER,** SO I'D BETTER CHECK UP.

10-27 DIST. BY POST-HALL SYNDICATE.

WELL! THERE'S THE LOYAL PAL OF THE LOYAL RUNAWAY CANDIDATE! ARE **YOU** RUNNIN' OUT TOO, YOU **LOYAL** CITIZEN?

HA! WE **EX-COWBIRDS** DON'T GIVE **OUR** LOYALTY EASILY.

RIGHT! IN FACT, FOR SOMETIME NOW WE AIN'T GIVE IT AT ALL!

WUMP!

COPR 1952 WALT KELLY

UNCLE BALDWIN WILL GOTTA WAIT. THINK I'LL LOOK UP POGO.

OCTOBER 28, 1952

DOES YOU *GIVE UP?* DOES YOU ADMIT YOU ISN'T **POGO?**

MEMO TO EL FAKIR: THE SCOUNDREL IS TRYING TO EMBEZZLE OUR WARD'S DOWRY. THROW HIM IN THE RIVER. SIGNED: *F. Olding Munny.*

10-28 DIST. BY POST-HALL SYNDICATE.

OOP?

A GOOD IDEA!

HEY! HEY! THAT MEMO WASN'T TO **YOU!**

YOU DIDN'T SAY WHICH SCOUNDREL.

*HOW*EVER, I APOLOGIZE!

COPR 1952 WALT KELLY.

OCTOBER 29, 1952

OCTOBER 30, 1952

OCTOBER 31, 1952

NOVEMBER 1, 1952

POGO by Walt Kelly

NOVEMBER 5, 1952

Panel 1:
A *VICTORY!* A *VICTORY!* A MORAL VICTORY! POGO LOST.

WHO WON?

Panel 2:
MMF.... IT'D BEEN BETTER DID *POGO* WIN ···· COULD OF SPELT IT OUT EASIER ···· THIS NAME GOT "N" IN IT, AN' A "O" AN' A FEW OF THEM "E"s ···· GOT "S" IN HER, TOO.

"T" TOO?

Panel 3:
YESSIR! DON'T MIND IF I *DO!* THIS FELLOW SEEMS LIKE A BOY WHAT WRIT A BOOK ONCE.

OH, THE MAN WHAT GIVED HIS *BIRTHDAY* AWAY TO THE LI'L' GAL WHAT WAS BORN ON *CHRISTMAS DAY?*

Panel 4:
WELL, *NO!* NOT EXACTLY *HIM* ···· THE *OTHER* ONE ····· AN' *HE'S* BEEN A *WINNER BEFORE.*

I *ALWAYS* SAID: *CASEY O'STENGEL* WOULD MAKE A *GREAT* PRESIDENT.

11-5   DIST. BY POST HALL SYNDICATE.

COPR 1952 WALT KELLY

NOVEMBER 6, 1952

Panel 1:
THING FOR POGO TO DO IS KEEP ON RUNNIN' FOR THE NEXT *FOUR* YEARS. COME *1956* HE WILL HAVE PILED UP *E*-NOUGH VOTES TO CARRY *BOTH* THE *NORTH* AN' *SOUTH AMERICAN* COUNTENANCE.

Panel 2:
COUNT-ENANCE?

HE MEANS *CONT-INENTS.*

Panel 3:
JES' WHAT I SAYS ... COUNTENANCE.

I LIKES PEOPLE WHO AIN'T AFEARED TO USE *BIG* WORDS.

Panel 4:
COME WHAT MAY.

RIGHT.

11-6

DIST. BY POST HALL SYNDICATE.

COPR 1952 WALT KELLY

14

POGO

by Walt Kelly

NOVEMBER 7, 1952

Panel 1: IF YOU GOT NOTHIN' *EXCITIN'* OR *AMAZIN'* PLANNED LIKE THE EVENTS OF THE PAST FEW WEEKS I BELIEVE I'LL VISIT MY UNCLE *BALDWIN* ...

OKAY.

Panel 2: HE IS ALWAYS WORRYIN' ABOUT LOSIN' HIS *HAIR.*

WELL, AT *HIS* AGE, HE AIN'T GOT MUCH ELSE TO DO.

Panel 3: *WHOOSH!* WHERE'D YOU GIT THE *OUTFIT*?

NONE OF YOUR *NEEDLENOSIN'* BUSINESS.

Panel 4: WAS THAT *YOU*?

DON'T BELIEVE IT *WAS* ..... I AIN'T GOT *NO* HAT LIKE THAT.

COPR 1952 WALT KELLY

11-7 DIST. BY POST HALL SYNDICATE.

NOVEMBER 8, 1952

Panel 1: BEFORE YOU GO OFF TO VISIT YOUR *BALD* UNCLE, BALDWIN, MEBBE YOU'D *BETTER* FIND OUT WHO IS THIS PORKYPINE THAT LOOKS LIKE YOU.

WELL, I DUNNO.

11-8 DIST. BY POST HALL SYNDICATE.

Panel 2: BUT HE'S A *STRANGER.* DON'T YOU WANT TO KNOW HIM?

ONE OF ME IS ABOUT *ALL* I KIN STOMACH.

Panel 3: BESIDES, I IS ANXIOUS TO GIT THIS PRESENT TO UNCLE BALDWIN *SOMETHIN'* TO KEEP HIS HAIR IN ..... IT'S KIND OF A JOKE ... *ROUSES* SOME FOLKS.

HE CAN KEEP IT IN A JAR ... HA HA?

Panel 4: YEP! ONLY IN *WATER* ... THEN, LIKE HORSE HAIRS, THEY CHANGE TO *SNAKES* ... AN', SINCE THEY IS *HIS* PERSONAL SNAKES, HE CAN TRAIN 'EM TO NESTLE ON HIS HEAD LIKE A WIG ... SHOULD BE MIGHTY COOL.

NATURAL WAVY, TOO.

COPR 1952 WALT KELLY

NOVEMBER 10, 1952

NOVEMBER 11, 1952

NOVEMBER 12, 1952

NOVEMBER 13, 1952

NOVEMBER 14, 1952

NOVEMBER 15, 1952

NOVEMBER 17, 1952

NOVEMBER 18, 1952

19

NOVEMBER 19, 1952

I IS BEEN GOIN' OVER MY PAST, POGO, AN' UP TO NOW I IS *NEVER* DOUBTED I WAS *ME*.

THERE'S THE FELLER WHAT *LOOKS* LIKE YOU. SEEM'S IF HE'S A-PULLIN' OUT.

A-HOY!

SIR, THIS PLACE IS ONLY SWAMP ENOUGH TO HOLD *ONE* OF US....

WELL, THIS IS A MIGHTY DECENT GESTURE.

RIGHT! HERE'S A BAG PACKED FOR YOU.....MY ADVICE IS FOR YOU TO HEAD OUT *BRESH COUNTRY WAY*--- OFF TO DODD COUNTY OR SOME PLACE.

COME ON OVER WHEN *YOU* WANTS, POGO --- I IS BAKED A CAKE.

NOVEMBER 20, 1952

THAT PORKYPINE WAS MIGHTY NICE, PACKIN' ME A BAG SO'S I COULD GO AWAY.

MEBBE HE IS *YOU*... HE GOT A GOOD HEART ON HIM.

FIGGER I MOUGHT OF PACKED A SAN'WICH OR TWO INSIDE?

OPEN HER UP AN' SEE IF THEY *IS* SOME LUNCH.

DESIST-- I AIN'T TO *EAT!* ... I'M A PASSENGER.

LUMPY LOU, THE *FAT FROG!* IN THERE JES' TO *HEAVY* UP THE BAG.

NARY A CRUMB NOR A STITCH ELSE.

THAT *OTHER* PORKYPINE SOLD ME A TICKET TO FARAWAY PLACES. A LUXURY CRUISE... RECLININ' CHAIRS..... FREE SELTZER! HOW FARAWAY IS

I... WHERE IS THE SODA?

20

POGO

by Walt Kelly

NOVEMBER 21, 1952

NOVEMBER 22, 1952

NOVEMBER 24, 1952

NOVEMBER 25, 1952

POGO by Walt Kelly

NOVEMBER 26, 1952

I BEEN THINKIN'... THAT OTHER FELLA AIN'T **UNCLE BALDWIN.**

HE MEBBE IS RIGHT...THE SWAMP GOT ONLY ROOM ENOUGH FOR **ONE** SOUR PUSS.....I BETTER GO ON OFF....I CAN'T TELL IF **HE'S** PORKY OR **I** IS.....BUT I **DO** KNOW IT DON'T PAY TO CROWD UP A PLACE WITH **PORKYPINES.**

EVENTUALLY **EVER'** MAN GOTTA FACE THE PROBLEM OF TRYIN' TO FIGGER IF IT'S **WORTH-WHILE** TO PROVE THAT HE **IS** HIMSELF.

G'BYE

NOVEMBER 27, 1952

DING BING IT! JES' WHEN A MIGRATORY MAN NEEDS A FISH, IT STARTS TO **RAIN!** THEM FISH AIN'T GONE BITE **NOW**... GIT HAULED OUT AN' GIT ALL WET.

THEY'S DOWN BELOW SITTIN' ROUN' THE **FIRE** TELLIN' LIES 'BOUT THE **BIG FISHERMENS** WHO ALMOST CAUGHT 'EM----AN' I AIN'T GONE SIT OUTSIDE HERE----

...GITTIN' SOAKED TO THE **SKIN** OFFERIN' **UNREQUITED** LOVE TO A MESS OF INDOOR, **UNSPORTIN'**, **SUMMER** SOLDIERIN', SEDENTARY, PISCATORY **PUSSY FOOTERS!** THEY KIN **DIG** THEIR **OWN** WORMS.

NOVEMBER 28, 1952

NOVEMBER 29, 1952

DECEMBER 1, 1952

DECEMBER 2, 1952

DECEMBER 3, 1952

DECEMBER 4, 1952

26

DECEMBER 5, 1952

DECEMBER 6, 1952

DECEMBER 8, 1952

DECEMBER 9, 1952

DECEMBER 10, 1952

DECEMBER 11, 1952

POGO

by Walt Kelly

DECEMBER 12, 1952

DECEMBER 13, 1952

DECEMBER 15, 1952

DECEMBER 16, 1952

DECEMBER 17, 1952

DECEMBER 18, 1952

DECEMBER 19, 1952

DECEMBER 20, 1952

DECEMBER 22, 1952

DECEMBER 23, 1952

DECEMBER 24, 1952

DECEMBER 25, 1952

DECEMBER 26, 1952

DECEMBER 27, 1952

DECEMBER 29, 1952

DECEMBER 30, 1952

DECEMBER 31, 1952

JANUARY 1, 1953

POGO

by Walt Kelly

JANUARY 2, 1953

JANUARY 3, 1953

POGO

by Walt Kelly

POGO

JANUARY 7, 1953

JANUARY 8, 1953

POGO

by Walt Kelly

JANUARY 9, 1953

JANUARY 10, 1953

JANUARY 12, 1953

JANUARY 13, 1953

43

WHAT WAS THIS NEWS YOU RUN OVER TO TELL US'N, COUSIN?

AH, YES! WELL, YES..... AH-HUM--MMP. ...NEWS.... WELL, NOW, -HMM....

I REMEMBER! THEM TWO ON THE OUTSIDE PULLED OFF THE HEAD OF THAT BOY IN THE MIDDLE!

1-14
DIST. BY POST HALL SYNDICATE.

COPR. 1953 WALT KELLY

I'M GLAD IT WAS A MOP WE PULLED OFF THE HANDLE AN' NOT YOUR HEAD OFFA YOU, UNCLE BALDWIN.

IT'S A COMFORT

ME AN' OWL COMED AROUND TO GIT YO' TO SWEAR OFF KISSIN' MIZ MA'M'SELLE DURIN' 1953----

SHHH SHH

WELL, I...UM...

SHHH! SH! THE BOY BIRD WATCHERS IS HOLDIN' WINTER MANEUVERS.

SHHH... WE IS TRAILIN' A PTARMIGAN.

SH! AN' OL' PEEK-ABOU BEN ADHEM LEADS ALL THE REST.

EVER SEE A PTARMIGAN?

SEE ONE! I CAN'T EVEN SAY ONE.

1-15 DIST. BY POST HALL SYNDICATE.

COPR. 1953 WALT KELLY

44

JANUARY 16, 1953

JANUARY 17, 1953

45

JANUARY 19, 1953

JANUARY 20, 1953

46

JANUARY 21, 1953

JANUARY 22, 1953

47

JANUARY 23, 1953

JANUARY 24, 1953

JANUARY 26, 1953

WISH YOU COULD REMEMBER WHAT YOU DID WITH THAT *MILLION*.

ON ACCOUNT OF MY RECENT *ILLNESS* I CAN'T RECALL EVEN *HAVIN'* IT.

BUT I TOLD YOU OF A *SECRET INGREDIMENT* TO SELL TO HOUSEWIFES..... SOMETHIN' THEY *GOTTA* HAVE AFORE THEY EVEN *KIN START* TO CLEAN.

FOR THIS SECRET YOU WAS GONNA GIVE ME *HAFFA* YOUR MILLION.!

I CAN'T EVEN FIND *MY* HALF. EASY COME · EASY GO —— SO I'LL BE FAIR.

I'LL GIVE YOU *BACK* THE NAME OF THE SECRET INGRED. IMENT.....*LISTEN CLOSE NOW*, IT'S *DIRT* ···· GET IT? HELLO, UNCLE BALDWIN, ARE YOU THERE? IT'S *DIRT*... D LIKE IN *DIRT*... I LIKE IN DIRT R LIKE IN DIRT... T LIKE IN ORANGE PEKOE.

JANUARY 27, 1953

H'LO CHURCHY AN' UNCLE BALDWIN, IS YOU DIGGIN' *BAIT?*

NO, POGO. US IS DIGGIN' OUR *FORTUNE*.

BUT IT'S SUCH A *POW'FUL SECRET*....

WE CAN'T TELL YOU WHAT WE IS PUTTIN' IN THESE BOXES TO SELL TO *HOUSEWIFES* ----US *MIS*LAID MY *MILLION* DOLLARS AN'

TO GIT IT BACK, US IS GONE MAKE *BILLIONS* SELLIN' THIS STUFF TO *HOUSEWIFES* 'CAUSE THEY NEEDS IT AFORE THEY GOTTA USE SOAP AN' WATER EVEN....

WHY, *THAT'S* DIRT!

YOU MUST OF TOLE!

HMM-- *DIRT!* WODDYA KNOW?!

49

POGO

by Walt Kelly

JANUARY 28, 1953

FIRST PERSON US'LL CALL ON WITH THE UNDISPENSABLE INGREDIMENT WILL BE A OL' FRIEND --- I'LL SHOW YOU HOW TO APPROACH WIMMENS...

WATCH HOW I SWEEPS HER OFF'N HER *FEETS.*

You!

GOOD AFTERNOON (SMEERP) I WONDER IF I COULD HAVE A FEW MINUTES OF YOUR TIME... *SMEERP!*

WHAT HAPPENED?

UNCLE BALDWIN WAS GONE SHOW ME HOW TO IMPRESS HOUSEWIFES BUT MIZ MAM'SELLE HAD A LONG-HANGLE BRUSH AN' HE WAS *CARPLED* AWAY.

PHOO ON PLAYIN' THE *GENT'MAN* --- I SHUNTNA TOOK OFF MY HAT.

DIST. BY POST HALL SYNDICATE
1-28

COPR 1953 WALT KELLY

JANUARY 29, 1953

THERE THEY GO -- NOT TELLIN' WHAT THEIR SECRET *INGREDIMENT* IS.

DIST. BY POST-HALL SYNDICATE
1-29

'LONG AS THEY'S SHOWIN' IT *ONLY* TO HOUSE WIFS, *US WILL BE HOUSE-WIFS* ...COME ON!

NICE PLACE YA GOT HERE, OWL.

THANKS.

COPR 1952 WALT KELLY

'TAINT MINE REALLY... IT'S *POGO'S.* ONLY MODERN ONE IN THE SWAMP... *BEADED PORTIERES* ... NEW FANGLE WHALE OIL LAMPS.... *WAX FRUIT BOWL* AN' *ALL* .....

50

POGO
by Walt Kelly

JANUARY 30, 1953

JANUARY 31, 1953

51

FEBRUARY 4, 1953

FEBRUARY 5, 1953

FEBRUARY 6, 1953

FEBRUARY 7, 1953

FEBRUARY 9, 1953

FEBRUARY 10, 1953

FEBRUARY 11, 1953

FEBRUARY 12, 1953

FEBRUARY 13, 1953

PSSST...AS A OLD FRIEND.....TELL ME.... WHAT'S YOU AN' UNCLE BALDWIN UP TO?

OH, I IS GONE OUTEN BUSINESS WITH **HIM**.. ALBERT GOT SUCH A GOOD PROPOSITION THAT **I** IS JOINED UP ON **HIM**!

UNCLE BALDWIN IS SELLIN' "*DIRT*" TO HOUSEWIFES (CAN'T START TO CLEAN 'LESSEN YOU GOT IT), AND HE OFFER ALBERT A BARGAIN IN *DIRT*.

DIRT!? AGAIN! HUMPH!

YEP, AN' OL' ALBERT KIN BUY A MILLION BOXES AT A ***PENNY OFF!*** RIGHT THERE HE'S AHEAD ***TEN THOUSAND DOLLARS!*** BLUB BUBBLUB BLUBLE

OL' ALBERT WOULD *IMMEDIATE* BE A **TEN THOUSANDAIRE**. SO WE GONE TAKE THE MONEY AN' *TRAVEL*.....OFF TO THE BERMOOTHES AN' WATCH THE **ONIONS** AN' THE **EELS**. .....HEY, WHERE YOU GOIN'?

PAH!

2-13   DIST. BY POST-HALL SYNDICATE.

COPR. 1953 WALT KELLY

FEBRUARY 14, 1953

HERE COME OL' POGO! UNCLE BALDWIN IS **GUV** HIM A BOX OF THAT *SECRET FORMULA*

HEIGHDY, KIND SIR! COULDST PRITHEE PITY AN' PARDON US AN' LOAN US THE BORRY OF THAT **BOX**?

SHONUF. YOU KIN HAVE IT **ALL**.

BALDWIN SAY IT'S GOOD TO **EAT**...BUT I DUNNO.

A **EXCELLENT** SUGGESTION. SEE, ITS **SECRET** IS GUARDED BY LABELING IT "*DIRT*." BUT WE CAN TASTE IT AN' SOLVE ITS *CIPHER*

BULLY.

UG-OOG.. SPTAH! I-(GUH) AIN'T-....YAK.... COTCHED ON TO NO INGRED-IMENTS YET.

IF I WASN'T A OLD SECRET INGREDIMENT TASTER I'D **SWEAR** IT WAS DIRT.

2-14   DIST. BY POST-HALL SYNDICATE.

COPR. 1953 WALT KELLY

POGO

by Walt Kelly

FEBRUARY 16, 1952

I BEEN TASTIN' THIS "DIRT" FOR TWO DAYS AN' I CAN'T TELL WHAT IS ITS SECRET INGREDIENT

IT GOT A KINDA GRITTY SANDY KINDA FLAVOR ON IT AN'...

YOWP! MY TEETH! I CRUNKED ON A WALNUT!

CRUNK!

LOOK AT THE LUNKS THEY LEFT IN THAT STUFF.....I OUGHT TO SUE THE PURE FOOD DEPARTMENT...

HEY!

YOU BIT DOWN ON A GOLD NUGGET! YOU IS STRUCK PAY DIRT!

MMM?

FEBRUARY 17, 1952

THAT NUGGET YOU CRUNCHED ON MUST OF COME FROM HERE ...THIS IS THE SPOT WHERE THEY DUG!

THE SECRET INGREDIMINT IS GOLD! AN' WE'LL BE RICH RICH RICH RICH!

RICH? THAT NUGGET WAS MY OWN STORE BOUGHTEN GOLD MOLAR OF 14 KARAT BRASS ALL THE WAY FROM ST. AUGUSTINE.

CAREFUL! STEADY! STEADY! YOU'LL DISSOLVE OUR PARTNERSHIP.

LETTIN' ME DIG ALL THAT WHILE! AN' FER BRASS!

58

FEBRUARY 18, 1953

FEBRUARY 19, 1953

FEBRUARY 20, 1953

FEBRUARY 21, 1953

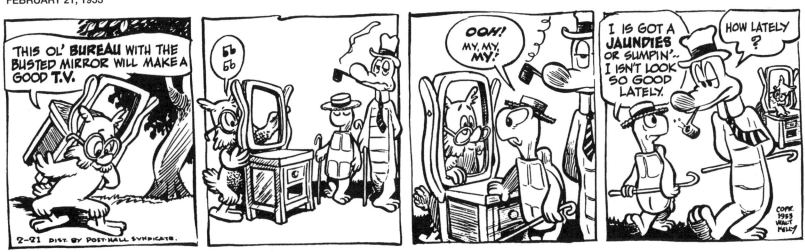

FEBRUARY 23, 1953

FEBRUARY 24, 1953

FEBRUARY 25, 1953

FEBRUARY 26, 1953

FEBRUARY 27, 1953

FEBRUARY 28, 1953

POGO by Walt Kelly

MARCH 2, 1953

You see anything of an incomin' liner with a friend of mine aboard, Pogo?

NOPE

You sure? He's a mole by trade ~~~ squinty look on him ~~~ nobility stamped all over him ~~~~

WHAT'D THEY DO *THAT* FOR?

Probably wearin' a sports coat ~ might have a spray gun with him ~~~ he's very hygienic ~ You sure you've looked sharp?

I LOOK SHARP AS MOST... .....LINERS DON'T COME IN HERE.

COPR 1953 WALT KELLY

Ha! That's all you know! Here comes the Hon. Mole now. Huzzah, friend, huzzah, I say!

SORRY, DEAC...HAD TO COME IN BY SECOND CLASS CABIN.

3-2   DIST. BY POST HALL SYNDICATE

MARCH 3, 1953

IS *THAT* YOUR FRIEND, THE MOLE, DEACON?

Right! In the flesh! The Hon. Mole MacCarony here to help with the Spring Bird Watching!

3-3   DIST. BY POST HALL SYNDICATE.

YESSIRREE INDEED! CAME ASHORE AT **WACCA PILATKA**, MUCH BETTER KNOWN AS **JACKSONVILLE**.

SHAKE HANDS, MR. MacCARONY, AN' WELCOME TO ~~ UMP..

WACCA PILATKA WAS NOT A TRUE AMERICAN NAME... BEING **MOSTLY** SEMINOLE... BETTER IT'S RENAMED.

COPR. 1953 WALT KELLY.

Sorry, Mole is quite sanitary minded, Pogo.

GERMS ARE EVERYWHERE, SIR. GERMS OF ALL NATIONS SWARM *UNCHECKED* THRU THE ENTIRE AIR! A *TRAVESTY.*

MARCH 4, 1953

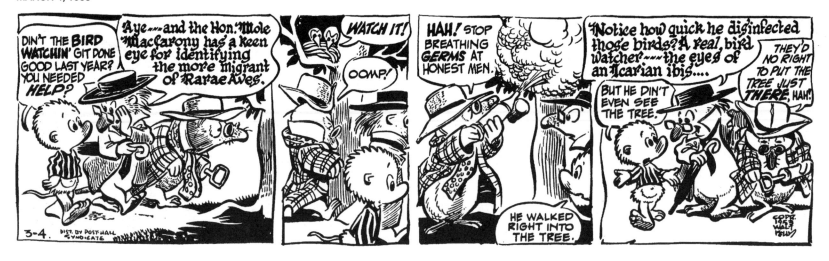

MARCH 5, 1952

MARCH 6, 1953

MARCH 7, 1953

POGO

by Walt Kelly

MARCH 9, 1953

MARCH 10, 1953

POGO
by Walt Kelly

MARCH 11, 1953

MARCH 12, 1953

MARCH 13, 1953

MARCH 14, 1953